YOUR GUIDE TO GET INTO MEDICAL SCHOOL

Practical Advice by
Trusted Professionals

Your Guide to Get into Medical School

Published by Aly Madhavji

Copyright © 2016 Jiayi Hu, Manveen Puri, Sameer Masood, and Aly Madhavji

License Notes: This book may be reproduced, copied and distributed for non-commercial purposes, provided the book remains in its complete original form.

Available from Amazon.com, CreateSpace.com, and other retail outlets. Information on how to obtain the **FREE eBook edition** can be found at the websites below or by scanning the QR code:

Website 1: **www.GuideToMed.com**

Website 2: **www.YourGuideToMed.com**

Facebook: **www.Facebook.com/Guide.To.Med**

Series Website: **www.YourGuideToSeries.com**

ISBN: 978-1-5368146-7-5 paperback

ISBN: 978-1-3706160-5-3 Smashwords

ISBN: 978-0-9921028-1-4 eBook and pdf

Special thank you to our support network, mentors, contributors, editors, friends, and family who helped make this book a reality. This book would not have been possible without your support. We appreciate you taking the time to read this guide.

Contributors

Written by

Jiayi Hu, MD
Manveen Puri, MD, CCFP
Sameer Masood, MD
Aly Madhavji, CPA, CA, CMA, CIM

Associate Editors

Bharat Bahl, MD, CCFP
Emergency Physician
University of Ottawa, Canada

Manpreet Basuita, MD Candidate
University of Toronto, Canada
Class of 2019

Kevin Brophy, MSc, MD, CCFP
Family Physician
University of Toronto, Canada

Anissa Capilnean, MSc, PharmD
Intensive Care Pharmacist
McGill University Health Centre, Canada

Kevin Chen, MD
Internal Medicine Resident
University of Manitoba, Canada
Class of 2020

James Chien, MD Candidate
University of Lublin, Poland

Ariel Gershon, MD Candidate
University of Western Ontario, Canada
Class of 2019

Colleen Foster, MD
Internal Medicine Resident
University of British Columbia, Canada
Class of 2019

Mitchell Huynh, BSc, BComm, MBA
Wealth Advisor

Romesa Khalid, MD
Family Medicine Resident
McMaster University, Canada
Class of 2017

Jessica Leen, MD
Internal Medicine Resident
Subspecializing in Clinical Pharmacology
University of Toronto, Canada
Class of 2018

Milad Modabber, MD
Ophthalmology Resident
McGill University, Canada
Class of 2019

Nicodemus Oey, MD, PhD
House Officer
SingHealth, Singapore
Class of 2018

Cristina Olteanu, MD Candidate
University of Toronto, Canada
Class of 2017

Ridah Ratanshi, BSc Candidate
Biomedical Sciences
University of Waterloo, Canada
Class of 2017

Tetyana Rogalska, MSc, MD
Family Medicine Resident
University of Ottawa, Canada
Class of 2018

Shahnur Saiyad, M.Biotech, DO Candidate
Michigan State University, United States
Class of 2017

Susan Shah, HBA
University of Toronto, Canada

Miliana Vojvodic, MSc, MD
Plastic Surgery Resident
University of Toronto, Canada
Class of 2019

Jay Wang, MD
Psychiatry Resident
University of British Columbia, Canada
Class of 2019

Aaron Wong, MBBS
Radiology Registrar
Monash Health, Australia
Class of 2021

Andrew Wong, MD Candidate
Wayne State University, United States
Class of 2018

Vincent Wu, MD Candidate
Queen's University, Canada
Class of 2018

Foreword

It is commonly known that the application process to medical school is competitive. From our experience, about 1% of students who express an interest in becoming a physician during their first year of undergraduate studies, eventually matriculate into medical school.[1] While pursuing a career in medicine remains a dream for many and is considered the endpoint of a journey, many different paths can lead towards that destination.

Given the significant time commitment required for a successful application, the decision to pursue medicine is one of the biggest decisions many high school and undergraduate students face. However, many applicants do not look beyond gaining the coveted admission letter and are then left with an incomplete understanding of what medical school entails, and the diverse career paths they can take after obtaining their MD. One of the primary reasons for this is that despite significant progress made in recent years, medicine remains a "closed

---

[1] In the absence of any scientific studies that have measured this data, the 1% figure is an estimate based on admissions data and the personal experiences of the authors. We know admissions data indicates that approximately 14% of applicants to medical school in Ontario matriculate into medical school. We also estimate that less than 10% of the students who think about pursuing medical school during their first year of undergraduate studies eventually end up applying to medical school due to a range of reasons, including guidance and academics.

door" career. A large proportion of students in our medical class had at least one immediate relative within the profession, which is also reflected in the literature.[2] The barriers created by such exclusivity make it difficult for those who have not been socialized into the profession from a young age to navigate the unspoken pitfalls of the admissions process.

This book attempts to break down some of those barriers. It focuses on every component of the medical school application process. It differs from the many other books written on this subject by taking an experiential approach. We believe that the best way to learn about medical school acceptance is to garner advice from those who have recently achieved that milestone, as well, as from individuals in related professions who can provide valuable insights.

This guide is divided into ten chapters, each of them covering an important step along a premed's journey. While this book has a focus on North America, we have written this guide with a global audience in mind, as many of the concepts discussed are relevant to any medical school application process. As such, although the key components of the application process to medical school remain the same across various training systems, not every chapter will be equally relevant to every

---

[2]Simmenroth-Nayda A., Gorlich, Y., Medical school admission test: advantages for students whose parents are medical doctors? MBC Medical Education. 15: 81. 2015.

reader. Typically, an application is composed of academic performance, volunteer activities, research projects, medical college admission test performance, and extracurricular activities.

We have combined the prescriptive style of most books of this type with detailed stories of how real people navigated their personal journeys to reach successful outcomes. This guide shares a broad range of perspectives on what it takes and means to be a physician. We are more convinced than ever that amongst applicants who have the academic credentials, those who seek mentors and network early within the profession, be it through family or friend circles, and those who learn from their mistakes are accepted earlier. This book will help you in that journey towards medical school acceptance and an exciting career in medicine!

Jiayi Hu, MD
Manveen Puri, MD, CCFP
Sameer Masood, MD
Aly Madhavji, CPA, CA, CMA, CIM

Table of Contents

Contributors 3

Foreword 6

Chapter 1: Academics 11
1.1 Staying focused and achieving academic excellence 11
1.2 Choosing the right undergraduate program and courses 14

Chapter 2: Volunteering 17
2.1 Being the best volunteer you can be 17
2.2 Volunteering abroad 19
2.3 What does a meaningful volunteer experience look like? 21

Chapter 3: Research 23
3.1 The nine essential secrets for getting involved in research 23
3.2 Pursuing research abroad during your summers 28
3.3 Completing an undergraduate thesis project 30

Chapter 4: Performing your best on the Medical College Admission Test 32

Chapter 5: Extracurricular activities 36
5.1 Getting involved in extracurricular activities 36
5.2 Managing time between academics and extracurricular activities 39
5.3 Leadership 42

Chapter 6: Non-traditional background before medical school 47
6.1 Engineering 47
6.2 Graduate studies 49
6.3 Pharmacy 53

Chapter 7: International students 55
7.1 Studying medicine in North America as an international student 55
7.2 Obtaining a study visa 57

Chapter 8: Interviews 60
8.1 Medical school interviews 60

Chapter 9: Medical school and beyond 67
9.1 The medical school curriculum and residency match 67
9.2 Matching to Canada for residency as a US medical student 69
9.3 Residency and fellowship 71
9.4 Working as a Medical Officer in the military 75
9.5 Physician turned entrepreneur 78

Chapter 10: Building your soft skills 80
10.1 Personal branding 80
10.2 How to network 82
10.3 Take a leap of faith & learn how to bounce back from failure 85

Top 10 take home messages 87

References 89

About the authors 92

Chapter 1: Academics

1.1 Staying focused and achieving academic excellence

By Anne Guo, HBSc, MD

Anne graduated from the Laboratory Medicine and Pathobiology program at the University of Toronto in 2010 with the highest GPA in her college. She subsequently completed her MD from Queen's University in Kingston in 2014 and is now pursuing residency training in Anaesthesia in Germany (Class of 2020). In this piece, Anne discusses the tools required for academic excellence.

I once came across an article on maintaining a successful relationship. It was filled with elegantly thought out pieces of advice, backed by years of research from psychologists and sociologists. It reminded me of the trials and tribulations of a pre-med student. Over the years, I have gotten to know many medical students and I can share a few lessons that we have learned through our collective personal experiences.

1. Success does not fall from the sky — find out in advance how you will be evaluated

Do you want to impress a total stranger? Then you have to go the extra mile and do your homework. It is up to you to search for the exact criteria that will be used to evaluate you, either for courses during your undergraduate studies, or throughout the admissions process. What would score more points? Acquaint yourself with what is expected early on, so that there are no unpleasant surprises. When you want something that is not readily available, you need to be bold, creative, and take the initiative. The importance of each criterion may differ from school to school, but being prepared and knowledgeable on the details will help set you up for success.

2. Medical schools like to play hard-to-get — do not give up without a fight

Not everything needs to happen the way you had wished on your first try. Love at first sight certainly sounds romantic, but in many cases, we have friends who thought the world was ending after a breakup and are now living a happy life. The same applies to the admissions process. It's painful when we are rejected after having sacrificed so much of our youth to pursue the dream of becoming a doctor; hours of lost sleep to study in the library or trade the summer sun for the fluorescent light of the lab bench. It is heartbreaking to be rejected, but your hard work is not in vain. Try again and do not give up. A significant number of medical students enter through non-traditional paths, many of whom only succeed due to persistence. Be prepared to be persistent; applying to medical school is a great time investment, but remember that perseverance pays off.

3. Do not take advice from others for granted — learn to filter and decide for yourself

In light of a good GPA, no standard formula guarantees success. Somebody may tell you astronomy is a "bird" course to take, but you may have very little interest in extraterrestrial bodies that the course may become the bane of your existence! I truly admire the "super-humans" who volunteer overseas while publishing many papers, but rest assured that the majority of people get into medical school without having to set foot outside of their home countries to volunteer. Perhaps you may not be a good match for one particular university, but the reality is that you cannot please everybody. Find the right school that values you. At times, people share their success stories, but the important part is not to merely mimic it, but to find the right pieces of advice to create your own personal success story. Your story should highlight your strengths, accomplishments, and your personal roadmap forward.

1.2 Choosing the right undergraduate program and courses

By Cristina Olteanu, HBSc, MD Candidate (Class of 2017)

Cristina obtained her HBSc in Human Biology from the University of Toronto in 2012 and is currently an MD Candidate at the same institution (Class of 2017). She has helped numerous students with course selection to reach their academic potential more effectively and to identify their career aspirations. Here she shares some thoughts on picking the right undergraduate program and courses.

Deciding on a program of study and selecting the right courses for an undergraduate degree has been described by many students as challenging, unnerving, and even daunting. If medicine is your calling, you should apply to medical school regardless of your undergraduate degree, as long as you have all the prerequisite courses. If you do not have the prerequisite courses, speak to medical schools for their input on which alternative courses you may take as substitutions in order to be exempted from these requirements. Once you fulfill the prerequisite requirements, let your passion and academic skills guide the rest of your course selection process.

Your undergraduate experiences should be fulfilling and exciting, but also challenging enough for personal growth. I took a variety of Human Biology courses, including genetics, physiology, and anatomy, simply because I enjoyed the subject and strongly felt that these courses would build a strong foundation for the study of medicine. Not only did they serve that purpose, but I also enjoyed each one of them.

Having said that, do not feel that you must take biology courses to be accepted; you can take courses in any number of fields because medical schools encourage students from diverse academic backgrounds to apply.

Getting into medical school is not a race, but rather a long journey that involves continual learning and growth. Do not be disappointed if you feel your chosen program of study is not working out for you. You can speak with your counselors or senior students about switching programs, or even take extra time to explore your passion further by pursuing a Masters or Ph.D. degree before medical school.

Another key aspect to consider is how your courses can help prepare you for alternate careers. Acceptance into medical school is competitive due to the high volume of candidates and not everyone will be accepted. Through your experiences during your undergraduate studies, you may find another career path that you are passionate about. Many prerequisites for medicine can also apply to other professional programs such as pharmacy, dentistry, and nursing. Therefore, you may wish to take into consideration the common prerequisites required for various professional programs. Knowing you have a viable backup plan will allow you to also focus your energy on plan B.

Most importantly, pick courses that you can excel at. This may involve doing some research by talking to senior students, mentors, and professors to fully understand the content and evaluation process for a course of interest. Ultimately, you need a competitive academic record of accomplishments for admission into medical school. In other words, a strong academic profile is a very important factor for medical school admissions committee. An important focus should be on fulfilling the academic prerequisites for the medical schools of your choice while picking courses that align with your professional and personal interests, all while achieving academic excellence.

Chapter 2: Volunteering

2.1 Being the best volunteer you can be

By Nancy Jiang, HBSc, MD

Nancy received her HBSc in Health Sciences from McMaster University in 2009 and MD from the University of Toronto in 2015. She is currently a radiology resident at McMaster University (Class of 2020). She was the recipient of the regional Best Volunteer Award from the Canadian Diabetes Association (2011).

Applying for medical school is a long and hard journey. Rest assured that it would be worth all your effort in the end! If you are thinking about medicine, having a good GPA alone is not enough. What distinguishes you are your extracurricular and volunteering experiences. Find an area that you are passionate about and get involved. For example, you can volunteer with a community organization or local chapter. National cardiovascular or cancer care associations are just some examples of organizations that have regional branches recruiting volunteers.

Here are five key points to keep in mind when identifying volunteer opportunities:

1. **Ask around** for volunteer opportunities; your friends, classmates, local community leaders, career centers at your school, etc. The chances are that there are always new

programs and projects starting. You can be the founding member of a new initiative, or take on a leadership role and work on an existing initiative.

2. **Work hard.** Show dedication and your passion for providing a service to helping others. Bring your heart and enthusiasm into the experience!

3. **Have fun.** "Volunteering should not feel like a chore." Consider your skill set and devise innovative ways to provide value to the community.

4. **Pick your activity wisely.** You need to consider your personal interests, areas for personal improvement, and your future career goals. Remember, volunteering is also a valuable opportunity for personal growth and networking. Spend some time to think about what the optimal activity for you will be.

5. **Most importantly, it benefits your community!** It is an excellent opportunity to experience the altruistic value of volunteering, which has a tremendous positive impact on personal growth and character.

2.2 Volunteering abroad

By Cristina Olteanu, HBSc, MD Candidate (Class of 2017)

Cristina obtained her HBSc in Human Biology from the University of Toronto in 2012 and is currently an MD Candidate at the same institution (Class of 2017). She has extensive volunteering experiences abroad in healthcare.

In order to genuinely understand and prepare for a career as a physician, I sought projects abroad that offered firsthand medical experiences. My first experience abroad in the healthcare field was at the age of 17 in India. I always had an interest in science and medicine and was looking for more opportunities to be exposed to medicine while in high school. It was an eye-opening experience to see medicine practiced in another country. I wanted to shadow physicians abroad so that I could make sure that medicine was the most suitable career path for me, regardless of where I choose to work in the future. Not only was this confirmed, but more experiences in Peru, Africa, and Argentina solidified my passion for medicine.

Overall, these experiences helped me realize that excellent communication skills with patients can make a difference. They further refined my knowledge of ethics in medicine and deepened my understanding of cultural issues in patient care. In addition, they helped me grow as a person, learn another language, and make the friends I keep in touch with to this day.

I also learned to consider the impact of our work on the community by asking myself: "Is this sustainable for this community?" While making contributions is significant, it is also essential to ensure that the community has the systems, infrastructure, and ability to be self-sufficient and continue the initiative after you progress to the next initiative.

Many students feel that they need to have experiences abroad to be competitive applicants for medical school. This is not true. Medical schools tend to value volunteering in their communities just as much. There are many opportunities to help those in need in your neighborhood; they might be much closer than you think! Whether it is it in your neighborhood or abroad, it is important to make a positive and lasting impact.

2.3 What does a meaningful volunteer experience look like?

By Henry Chen, HBSc, MSc, MD

Henry completed his HBSc in Laboratory Medicine and Pathobiology and his MSc in Nephrology at the University of Toronto (2010 and 2012, respectively). He will be pursuing Family Medicine residency at Queen's University (Class of 2018) after completing his medical degree in Toronto (Class of 2016). He enjoyed playing music in his spare time and helped start Mount Sinai Minstrels – a volunteer musician program at Mount Sinai Hospital in Toronto.

As a pre-med student, I was looking for meaningful hospital-based volunteer positions. Fortuitously, I met a student at a pre-med club who introduced me to the volunteer coordinator at Mount Sinai Hospital in Toronto, Canada. With time, I was able to recruit some friends from the *Hart House Symphonic Band* (where I was a flutist) and the *Hart House Chamber Strings* in Toronto. Together, the *Mount Sinai Minstrels* was born.

I am often asked if I still have time to play music during medical school. The answer is yes! Performing has always been an activity that I deeply enjoyed. Despite the academic demands of medical school, I always find time to play music as a way to relieve stress. In fact, I continued to perform at hospitals and soup kitchens. I also enjoyed playing music with other talented medical and allied health professional students in *Daffydil*, an annual charity musical show put on by students in the Faculty of Medicine at the University of Toronto. This is also an opportunity to meet many future colleagues in a non-academic setting.

I am a firm believer that music is therapeutic for patients. I cannot count the number of times that patients expressed how our music has brightened up their day. This is more than enough motivation for me to continue caring through the power of music.

Over the years, we have expanded from a team of seven members to over twenty. Our monthly mini-concerts now occur bi-weekly, and we are occasionally invited to play at other hospitals, as well. I still remember when we received a brand new piano donated from the community. We hope to continue to give back to the community for many years.

This experience is incredibly rewarding. You can seek other meaningful volunteering opportunities that demonstrate your unique passion and interests.

Chapter 3: Research

3.1 The nine essential secrets for getting involved in research

By Jiayi Hu, HBSc, MD

Jiayi completed numerous research projects at various academic institutions (University of Toronto, McGill University, University of Cambridge, and McMaster University) during medical school and residency. He enjoys both the basic and clinical science research. Here he shares a few thoughts on getting involved in research as an undergraduate student.

1. Start early. Nowadays, it is extremely rare to come across a medical school application without any research experience. This has almost become an unwritten requirement. During your undergraduate studies, there is limited time to conduct quality projects that yield meaningful results, especially considering the time required to overcome an initial learning curve. Therefore, it is important to take on research opportunities early. In addition, research plays a significant role during medical school and beyond.

2. Apply broadly. It is always difficult when applying for your first research position. The more positions you apply for, the higher the chances are of you securing at least one of them. Make sure you read through a professor's research interests and recent publications to demonstrate your interest in the field and to have the adequate background knowledge to discuss potential projects. In addition to a typical introductory email or phone call, you can also approach professors in person, for example, at networking events or attend professors' office hours, and discuss your research interests.

3. There are various opportunities to do research. Students typically get involved with projects during their summers. Remember that you may also be allowed to conduct a thesis project as an undergraduate course as explained in Section 3.3 "Completing an undergraduate thesis project" (typically done in your senior years). Also, you may become involved in survey-based research among your classmates that may not restrict you to a specific allotted time, such that you can maintain a flexible schedule. In addition, you can participate in studies in an administrative role, such as a research coordinator.

4. Be efficient. For basic science research, pick research projects/labs that have a quicker turnaround time for experiments given the research model or system at hand. For example, this may include microbiology studies (bacteria, yeast), DNA sequencing studies, and leukemia cell investigations among other models. This will allow you to generate more data in the limited time that you have for research.

5. Network locally and globally. In addition to building friendships with members of your lab or department, traveling is also a lot of fun in the summer! Simply apply for research positions at a location away from your home institution, as seen in the next section. The US, UK, and Germany usually have many summer research opportunities. One caveat is that it may be difficult to continue the project and carry it to completion after school starts again in the fall.

6. Pick the ideal lab. An ideal lab, in my opinion, should:

i. Place personal safety as top priority. This is very similar to the "non-maleficence" principle in medical ethics[3], which means, "do no harm" to achieve a possible beneficial outcome.

ii. Have a supportive and driven supervisor who is punctual and communicates with you on a regular basis.

iii. Have a cohesive and collaborative research team (including collaboration with other labs).

iv. Have a good publication record, which indicates that your research project will have a higher likelihood to be published.

v. Have an excellent team of technicians available to assist researchers.

vi. Have easy access to a biostatistician when necessary. Students often struggle to perform statistical analysis

---

[3]Gillon R., Medical ethics: four principles and plus attention to scope. British Medical Journal. 1994. 309: 184.

on their own and often resort to the expertise of biostatisticians.

vii. Allow for flexibility with research timelines, such that one can incorporate other academic or extracurricular activities into the schedule.

viii. Support for attending conferences and other networking opportunities, as students usually are not able to finance these opportunities on their own.

7. Strive for continuous improvement. Learn non-academic skills (leadership, communication, teamwork, conflict resolution, etc.) from your supervisor and other lab members. Research is not just about the project and the results, it is also about the interpersonal skills you gain from the interactions.

8. Be realistic and set realistic expectations, but work at your highest capacity.

Is it easy to publish a study? No, most projects will go unpublished during their expected or desired timeline. Some projects may never be published. However, there are many opportunities for you to display your research, such as conferences, student research days, and various online platforms.

Is your research going to change the world? Perhaps. However, the impact you make on your field of study will likely not be direct or immediate. Unfortunately, there is a substantial amount of research that is rarely read by the research community.

Is it going to help with your medical school application? In most cases, yes. The admissions committee will see your dedication and hard work in carrying out a research project. They will be curious to see if the scholarly and personal skills you have acquired can be brought forward as a future physician. Therefore, you must be able to effectively describe your research and the skills learned on both your application and during your interview.

9. Be reflective. Always evaluate your progress and make adjustments as necessary. Research findings can be unpredictable. Therefore, you should take a reflective approach throughout the research process and be flexible with your plans. Be open to feedback from others to help you improve your progress.

3.2 Pursuing research abroad during your summers
By Tetyana Rogalska, HBSc, MSc, MD

Tetyana completed her undergraduate studies and a Masters degree in Virology at the University of Toronto. She completed her medical degree at Queen's University (Class of 2016) and will be pursuing Family Medicine Residency at the University of Ottawa (Class of 2018). Here she shares her experience of doing summer research at Brigham and Women's Hospital in Boston, a fully affiliated teaching hospital of Harvard Medical School.

The field of medicine is driven by a collective desire to help the human condition, to restore function, and to give the patients we treat as much opportunity for fulfillment as possible. Incredibly, the limits to these possibilities are redefined every day, and it is this potential that drives my passion for clinical and translational research on wound healing. I became interested in this research opportunity because of my particular interest in wound healing. This fellowship offered an incredibly exciting opportunity to apply and build my skills in a stimulating and innovative environment, with international leaders in the field.

I learned many great things from this experience. One of them was the power of collaboration on a global scale. An evidently synergistic effect comes from working with individuals from different backgrounds and disciplines who are enthusiastic about exchanging ideas, perspectives, and experiences. It is not only motivating but also can lead you to discoveries you would never have made by working alone.

For future student applicants interested in research abroad, here are a few tips:

1. **Find your passion and follow it**. It requires determination, perseverance, and perhaps some traveling.

2. **Build skill sets that are important to you**. Whether specific (e.g. laboratory methods) or broad (e.g. leadership abilities), ask yourself, what skills do you need to be successful in your goals?

3. **Challenge yourself!** Getting out of your comfort zone is essential for personal growth. As a future medical student and physician, you must be prepared to deal with challenging situations on a day-to-day basis. The earlier you are exposed to these challenging situations, the quicker your personal development.

3.3 Completing an undergraduate thesis project

By Manveen Puri, HBSc, MD, CCFP, MPA Candidate (Class of 2018)

After completing an undergraduate thesis project in Cell Biology at the Hospital for Sick Children in Toronto during his third year, Manveen pursued a second undergraduate thesis project in his fourth year at the McLaughlin-Rotman Centre for Global Health in Toronto under the supervision of Dr. Peter Singer, a world-renowned expert in the field of global health. In this piece, Manveen discusses his motivation for pursuing research in global heath, what he learned, and the advice he has for students looking for similar research opportunities.

Global health is a broad field that draws on expertise from multiple disciplines, including the life sciences. Many of the grand challenges in global health require innovative technical solutions that a degree in the life sciences allows you to appreciate, especially since not everyone in the field is a scientist. However, it is important to remember that global health is truly a multidisciplinary endeavour and many ideas have failed to take off because of inadequate emphasis on political, cultural, and economic factors.

I was attracted to global health because it allowed me to ask broad questions on a global scale. Additionally, I had completed a thesis project in cell biology and wanted a different challenge. From a technical point of view, my global health project allowed me to gain experience in qualitative research that is widely used in medicine. I have since utilized those skills to complete another summer research project during medical school. On a more personal note, I learned that I was passionate about the social and cultural determinants of health and that I wanted to be able to make an impact on those in my future career.

Are you interested in pursuing a similar experience? I would suggest that you apply broadly for your first research position, since you will often need to take what you get. This may mean accepting a volunteer or part-time position that entails doing lab chores to get your foot through the door. I discovered this after receiving multiple rejections for a research position during my first summer. After being part of a few projects, you may be fortunate enough to choose your next position. Pursuing a thesis project is an ideal way to furtherdevelop and refine your research interests. As you progress in your research career, it becomes increasingly important to understand yourself and appreciate what truly excites you. Seek mentors and gain skills through varied experiences over a period. These experiences will help you decide on the role that research will play in your future career.

Chapter 4: Performing your best on the Medical College Admission Test

By Ariel Gershon, HBSc, MD Candidate (Class of 2019)

Ariel completed his HBSc in the Laboratory Medicine and Pathobiology program at the University of Toronto (Class of 2015). He is currently pursuing his MD at the Western University in London (Class of 2019). Over the years, Ariel has taught and mentored many students on the Medical College Admission Test (MCAT).

Most medical school admission processes require completion of a standardized exam to facilitate candidate selection. In the United Kingdom, there is the UK Clinical Aptitude Test (UKCAT). Similar exams in Australia include the Undergraduate Medicine and Health Sciences Admission Test (UMAT) and the Graduate Australian Medical School Admissions Test (GAMSAT). The North American version is the Medical College Admission Test (MCAT). We will focus on the MCAT, but similar information and resources may be available for other medical admission tests.

Do you want to do well on the MCAT? Well, you are in good company. Together with your GPA, your MCAT score is the primary determinant of your academic competitiveness to most medical schools. In 2015, the MCAT underwent a significant change. The new MCAT now includes content from the fields of psychology, sociology, and biochemistry. These changes can be a source of additional anxiety for those aspiring to become medical students. Do not fear! Fundamentally, the MCAT has not changed; at its core, it is still the same long multiple-choice test it has always been.

Since tutoring for the MCAT in 2010, I have seen many students achieve success and have deduced the habits that work. My goal here is to inform you of the strategies that are conducive to success and make you aware of resources that are available.

Start by reading the MCAT Essentials document[4] and the outline of the entire exam.[5] These two documents are produced by the AAMC (Association of American Medical Colleges) and will give you a good understanding of every topic and competency you will be responsible for on the MCAT. Use the second reference to guide your studying.

The MCAT is like a two-headed beast. First, there is a massive amount of content. Second, it requires precise reading and problem-solving skills that only come by actually practicing MCAT style questions. I have had many students who focused all of their time on content review and did not practice any problems. Do not make this mistake. Practicing questions is just as important as studying. The Critical Analysis and Reading Skills section (CARS, previously called "Verbal Reasoning") is an excellent example of the "problem solving" nature of the MCAT. It requires zero "content" knowledge. The only way to get better at CARS is to practice CARS passages. Similarly, the ability to solve other MCAT questions relies on practice.

At the very least, you should consider reviewing: (1) the official MCAT guide, (2) any AAMC full-length tests that have been released, (3) all the question packages that the AAMC has

---

[4] Association of American Medical Colleges. MCAT Essentials.
[5] Association of American Medical Colleges. MCAT Content.

produced, and (4) possibly additional full-length tests from a test preparation company. The Khan Academy is an excellent free resource with video lectures on all the content material of the MCAT, along with sample passages and questions with solutions. The Khan Academy has now officially collaborated with AAMC to develop new MCAT material. As such, the Khan Academy has around 100 passages for each of the three science sections on the exam, and additional passages for CARS. You may also consider obtaining content review books from a test preparation company. If you do purchase review content material, check with the AAMC outline to make sure that you have studied everything that may be on the MCAT.

Once you have collected all your study supplies, you must make a schedule. It will help you develop a pace at which you can get the most out of your prep material. Some suggestions for your study plan are to:

- Put your test date on the calendar and mark the day before as a rest day.

- Set one or two rest days each week.

- Every week, assign one full-length test (e.g. the AAMC full lengths, or others produced by prep companies). The next day will be dedicated to reviewing the full-length test just written.

- Dedicate the remaining study time to studying chapters from your content review books and your question books (e.g. the AAMC question pack). This will form the bulk of your schedule.

- Your schedule will vary depending on the material you have, preparation time, and your study style. I have outlined the basic framework. Do not worry if you are not able to complete the goals that you have set for yourself initially. Rather, you can and should revise your schedule based on your performance on practice tests. I made an example of a table that I produced with one of my students.[6]

Key things to remember:

- The MCAT is an essential prerequisite to medical school admission in North America. It is also accepted by other medical schools (such as Australia and the Caribbean) for North American applicants.

- Thoroughly read the information about the MCAT that the AAMC provides (the MCAT Essentials document and the official guide).

- The MCAT tests both your knowledge and your problem-solving skills. You should do enough practice problems and simulated full-length exams.

- Develop a study schedule and map out your exam date, simulated full-length exams, daily question sets, lectures to watch/read, and rest days. This will ensure that you are well prepared before your test date.

---

[6]Sample study schedule.

Chapter 5: Extracurricular activities

5.1 Getting involved in extracurricular activities
By Karen Chung, HBSc, MD

Karen obtained her HBSc (Health Sciences) at McMaster University in Hamilton and her medical degree from Queen's University in Kingston (Class of 2016). She will be pursuing Plastic Surgery residency at the University of Toronto (Class of 2021). She has been involved in and has co-founded numerous impactful student organizations. Here she discusses the importance of sharing one's passion with others.

Medical schools want to see a genuine person who excels at their commitments. Your undergraduate career is a time for exploration. Discover what you love and work on it. Then, take it a step further. One critical foundation for a medical career is a desire to help others. Use the knowledge and skills that you have gained from cultivating whatever hobby or interest you have and share it with others. Are you a soccer star? Mentor others who may not otherwise get the opportunity to play soccer. Are you a secret master chef? Consider volunteering at a soup kitchen or community nutrition program. Are you a social media expert? Some NGOs can likely use your expertise to advocate for the needs of the community. Are you musically inclined? Share your talents at a local nursing home, hospital, or school.

Are you excited yet? Here are three steps you can take to make sure your new initiative is effective:

1. Provide needs-based service

Most students intend to be helpful, but never ask how they should do it. Do not be that person. Before you go and change the world, take the time to figure out what needs are present in the area you are committed to. Do your research and talk to experts in the field. Talk to the people who will be impacted by the change. Share your ideas, especially with trusted friends and mentors. Go online to check if anyone else has had your idea and what he or she did to make it successful. Then troubleshoot! What problems did they come across? What problems will you encounter? Identify solutions before moving forward.

2. Work with others

The bigger the idea, the more likely you will need help. One risk of working with others is that they may not be as invested as you are, physically and emotionally. Therefore, take the time to share your vision to help them share it or identify those who have the same interests as you, and genuinely ask if they want to use their gifts to help others as well. People bring different skill sets and ideas to the table. If you have a solid idea of what you want to do, you should also be aware of the tools needed to make it a success. Look for people whose strengths can complement your weaknesses.

3. Make it sustainable

Congratulations! At this point, you have a feasible idea that will be useful to your community. What happens after you leave? This underscores the importance of working with others. You have the opportunity to be a mentor in addition to being a leader. Pay attention to someone who can potentially carry on this project if or when you leave and share what you learned.

Follow up with that person occasionally and see if you can provide any further guidance.

Leadership and problem-solving skills are extremely useful in a medical career. These are transferable skills you should continue to enhance and need to be highlighted in your applications and interviews. Investing time in an altruistic cause is an excellent way to develop those skills, while simultaneously pursuing your passion and having fun!

5.2 Managing time between academics and extracurricular activities

By Dominik Nowak, HBSc, MD

Dominik completed his undergraduate studies at the University of Toronto (Class of 2013), and his medical degree at McMaster University (Class of 2016). He will be pursuing Family Medicine residency at the same school (Class of 2018). He was also the captain of the McMaster's Men's Varsity Tennis Team (2015-2016). He will be sharing some tips on time management skills, and balancing academic and extracurricular activities.

I understand. You want to become a doc. You are tempted to hang up those ballet slippers and to close the piano drawer. In my case, I was tempted to put away the tennis racket. I needed stellar grades, those pristine reference letters, and that outstanding MCAT score. Each hour was valuable. The load does not get any lighter after getting into medical school; however, there are several reasons why you should continue pursuing high-level extracurricular activities throughout your undergrad and medical training.

First, I will offer an observation. Many of the best physicians have a passion outside of medicine. I once had a mentor tell me, "Dominik, to become a successful surgeon, you must stick to a strict schedule and never deviate from it. Spend your time either working/studying or sleeping." I immediately booted him from my list of mentors. Throughout my medical training, I have seen a recurring theme. The most balanced doctors who care and who go beyond for their patients are those with rich and fulfilling passions outside of work. They love their lives inside and outside of the clinic and the operating theatre. Strive to become one of those doctors.

The second observation is tangentially related to my first. The medical lifestyle can be tough. It is exhilarating, uplifting, and empowering. However, it is also draining. While you progress through your training, you will have many wonderful days and you will also have some lousy days. Whether you flunked a test or merely could not answer your supervisor's latest urological trivia, your self-esteem will inevitably take hits. It helps to have several spheres in which you can excel. You had a bad day in clinic...so what? It is still a good learning experience, and you still have many other talents that will help make you an excellent physician.

I am often asked how I manage senior medical student clinical duties with a varsity sport. I would say: one needs to prioritize, stays organized, and be committed in order to achieve a balance between various activities. It is also about working hard and making time for the things you love. You will usually wake up early, you will often get to bed late, and you will sometimes wonder how you manage with so little sleep. Playing tennis is part of who I am, and just as big of a role as being a medical student. There is no compromise to that.

Here are some strategies that have worked well for me to balance medical school and extracurricular activities:

1. A calendar app or an agenda is your best personal assistant.

2. Learn how to say "No." This may be difficult to do, but unless you have a time-turner, you may regret taking on

unnecessary commitments. It is better to do some things well than to stretch too thin and do many things poorly.

3. Take good care of yourself and remember to eat well, sleep well, and exercise! Seriously, balancing various activities and working hard means you need to take extra care of yourself.

4. Take rest days. Some days playing your sport will re-energize you. Playing eight days in a row, however, is a recipe for injury.

When I told my wise older brother of my acceptance into medical school, he said, "Dominik, never let medicine come in the way of your tennis." His facetious comment has plenty of truth. Therefore, I hope to pass this on to you…let medicine flourish as a passion of yours, and stay true to the other passions in your life.

5.3 Leadership

By Manveen Puri, HBSc, MD, CCFP, MPA Candidate (Class of 2018)

Manveen works as a Medical Officer with the Canadian Armed Forces and is a Family Physician who also practices rural Emergency Medicine. He has taken on various leadership roles over the years and has served on University of Toronto's Governing Council and as Chief Resident (Family Medicine) at Credit Valley Hospital in Mississauga. He has received both the Cressy Award and the Arbor Award for his continued leadership within the University of Toronto community.

Many national physician regulatory bodies establish a standardized set of competencies that a doctor must attain to be eligible for practice. In Canada, the Royal College of Physicians and Surgeons created the "CanMEDS" competency framework in the 1990's.[7] In 2015, CanMEDS underwent an update. Notably, the "manager" competency was updated to "leader." This was the only competency to undergo a name change in the 20-year history of CanMEDS. In justifying this change, the Royal College emphasized the importance of leadership skills in delivering high quality care within an increasingly complex healthcare system. While leadership has been extensively studied within the business and military communities, this level of emphasis on developing leaders represents a paradigm shift for medical education. Although leadership skills were always viewed as a valuable asset, they now have become a necessity. It will take years for this change to permeate a profession that has traditionally looked at direct individual patient care as its chief responsibility, and has left

---

[7] Royal College of Physicians and Surgeons of Canada. CanMEDS Framework.

"administration" to the reluctant few who were willing to take on the task. This change in Canada is in keeping with a global shift in expectations from medical professionals.

The fact that those leadership skills will even be more heavily scrutinized during the admissions process in the years ahead should come as no surprise to any premedical students. Nevertheless, there are many misconceptions about leadership, which persist. The following few paragraphs contain some leadership lessons that I have gathered along my journey.

1. Leadership is not an innate quality, but a skill

There is no doubt that some people have traits that make it easier for them to lead; however, like any skill, leadership can be improved with practice and effort. As premedical students, start developing those skills. Whether it is serving on the executive council of an extracurricular club or spearheading a new initiative, put yourself out there! Make mistakes and learn from them. Run for an elected position. It is okay if you lose! While there may be a role for formal leadership education (e.g. an MBA or courses through various physician executive and leadership organizations) at a later stage, you need to start somewhere. Leadership is more art than science, which means that it needs to be perfected with time.

2. Leadership can be developed in multiple settings

There are many different styles of leadership, and it helps to have a range of styles in your repertoire so that you can pick the right style to solve the problem at hand. It also means that it behooves you to seek out a range of leadership experiences, both formal and informal, to nurture those qualities. One of my most meaningful leadership experiences was being a one-to-one mentor to various high school students. It did not come with a fancy title, but the experience tremendously shaped how I have come to view myself as a leader. Many of you may already be good leaders after taking on significant responsibilities within a family or community setting while growing up. Do not let those skills fade just because you have moved away for university.

3. Seek out mentors and learn from them

There are excellent physician and non-physician leaders out there in healthcare and other related professions. Find out who these people are in your community and try seeking them out. You may be surprised to learn, as I was, that many of the best physician leaders are quite accessible and take it upon themselves to inspire and teach the next generation. Interacting with these individuals in person will at some level motivate you and can help you visualize what your career may look like. It is well known within the medical literature that you cannot teach the behaviours, values, and attitudes associated with becoming a physician through textbooks or lectures. Rather, these critical skills are transmitted from one generation to the next through role modeling and emulation.

While you may not always be able to access every desired mentor as a premedical student, you can nevertheless learn from their career paths through books, speeches, and talks. Below I have listed some books about physician career journeys and other resources that I found particularly useful.

- "Lessons Learned: Reflections of Canadian Physician Leaders" and "Leading from the front:

experiences of Canadian physician leaders". These two books contain vignettes from 31 physician leaders in Canada that chronicle their career paths and distil key reflections and decision points from a myriad of experiences. A must read![8]

- **American Association for Physician Leadership**: A one-stop shop for resources on physician leadership ranging from online modules to courses to opportunities for formal training.[9]

- **Canadian Medical Association Physician Leadership Institute**: This definitive Canadian database on physician leadership contains many free resources to get you started on your leadership journey.[10]

- **When Clinicians Lead**: This article explores the importance of physician leadership to improving healthcare systems and solving healthcare challenges around the world.[11]

- **Coaching Physicians to Become Leaders**: This article delves into the typical challenges facing physicians

---

[8]"Lessons Learned: Reflections of Canadian Physician Leaders" and "Leading from the front: experiences of Canadian physician leaders".
[9]American Association for Physician Leadership.
[10]Canadian Medical Association Physician Leadership Institute.
[11]When Clinicians Lead.

looking to take on leadership roles, and suggests how to get around common barriers.[12]

---

[12] Coaching Physicians to Become leaders.

Chapter 6: Non-traditional background before medical school

6.1 Engineering
By Fahad Chowdhury, B.Eng, M.Eng, MD (Class of 2013)

Fahad completed both his B.Eng and M.Eng in the field of engineering sciences at the University of Toronto, where he also completed his medical education (Class of 2013). He is an Internal Medicine resident with subsequent training as an Infectious Disease fellow at the University of Ottawa (Class of 2018).

I didn't always know that I wanted to pursue Medicine. In high school, I knew that I enjoyed math and physics, but I also enjoyed biology. Therefore, I started my educational journey at the University of Toronto's Engineering Science program with the intent of specializing in Biomedical Engineering. Through my undergraduate studies, I encountered the fast-paced field of biomedical research, specifically stem cell research. It was an exciting field to be involved in, one that was both innovative and had profound implications towards the betterment of patient care.

It was during this time spent in research that I realized that I wanted to help people, but in a more direct manner through medicine. I wanted to interact with individuals one-on-one and face-to-face. Also, I wanted to see first-hand the impact made by the past, current, and future medical advances. This motivated me to apply to medical school.

Although my path to medicine has been somewhat indirect, I am grateful and appreciative of the lifelong skills and aptitudes gained through my engineering program. In engineering, I learned to understand the basics of our most benign and complicated processes, both biological and otherwise. I learned how to explain complex findings based on the foundational principles, and then further build on them. I applied these logical steps to various projects: from coding, building robots to understanding signaling pathways of a genetically modified cell line. In the same manner, I can comprehend the different ailments that afflict the human body. This has taught me to be logical and inquisitive.

Engineering also allowed me to build on vital personal traits, which are required of me on a daily basis as a medical resident. Before university, I was shy. Engineering forced me to participate in group projects and present complex ideas by speaking in lecture halls filled with my peers or by compiling written reports with a team. I have learned how to become a better collaborator and communicator.

Overall, I would say my path to medicine has been adventurous, and I have been grateful for all my unique experiences that have brought me this far. I look forward to experiencing more encounters through a vibrant and life-changing career in medicine. Therefore, for those of you who are worried about not having followed a "traditional" premedical training program, do not lose hope because you can always apply the skills you learned into the practice of medicine.

6.2 Graduate studies

By Miliana Vojvodic, HBSc, MSc, MD (Class of 2014)

Miliana completed her HBSc at the University of Guelph before completing her MSc and MD at the University of Toronto. During her medical training, she was the Co-Editor-in-Chief for the Toronto Notes (30th Ed), a popular study resource for the LMCC (Licentiate of the Medical Council of Canada) Step 1 and USMLE (United States Medical Licensing Exam) Step 2 exams and the Essentials of Clinical Examination (7th Ed), an internationally published text for healthcare trainees. She is currently a Plastic Surgery Resident at the University of Toronto. Here she shares how a post-graduate degree can benefit one's medical education and beyond.

Many educational routes can lead aspiring physicians to their career of choice. In a knowledge economy, medical schools take advantage of the educational diversity and breadth of experiences within their student cohorts. Graduate students, in particular, have the asset of advanced research and critical thinking skills, which are viewed favourably in the competitive world of academic medicine. Furthermore, I would argue that the expertise, professionalism, and maturity of many graduate applicants are also coveted attributes.

Students who enter their medical studies with a Masters or Ph.D. degree will find their acquired skills to be easily transferable in an environment where fast-paced, independent learning is critical for success. Whether the ultimate career goal is to become a rural family physician or a sub-specialized clinician at a tertiary care center, entering medical school with a graduate degree in science offers an abundance of advantages for aspiring doctors.

1. Appraising medical evidence

Modern medicine is based on evidence, past and present. Medical school curricula are designed around the most fundamental principles across various specialties, provided in discreet packages or units for the benefit of the learner. Inherently, the information delivered to medical students is often the most distilled version of many years of research. The further along a medical student is in their studies, the more integral it will be to read and understand recent medical literature. During their clinical training years, students are exposed to rounds and journal clubs, where meaningful discussions are based on the latest landmark publications and clinical trials.

An experienced graduate student will know that not all published studies are equivalent and that there is variation in the level of evidence and the quality of research methods. Graduate students in the sciences have spent a significant amount of time appraising the literature, formulating critiques, and most importantly summarizing findings into the most important and validated points. Research methodology and statistical analysis may also be more familiar to graduate students.

It is also important to recognize the value of effective literature appraisal after completing medical school. Residents are encouraged to maintain a good understanding of landmark trials in their field and commonly analyze smaller studies for their practical relevance. Working physicians also need to maintain their credentials continuously by reviewing the new literature and applying updated guidelines and protocols in their practice.

2. Conducting original research

Medical students are encouraged to seek research opportunities throughout medical school. The goal of students and their respective supervisors is to conduct high-quality research that will influence their specialty through conference presentations and publications. In addition to acquiring research skills and proficiency in their field of study, completing a successful research project can be a significant advantage for the residency match and beyond. There are in fact very few reasons for avoiding research opportunities during medical school.

Designing a novel research project is an exciting challenge, but it also requires careful planning and foresight. Medical students with graduate degrees often have the necessary experience that allows them to work efficiently and independently, especially since time is scarce and expectations are high in medical school. Graduate students also often have a good network of colleagues and mentors for peer feedback on their research work. A trainee who can demonstrate a high level of independence in carrying a project from start to finish is a valuable asset to any supervisor.

3. Medical writing and publishing

An essential component of postgraduate training in the sciences and many other fields is the completion of a thesis and, in most cases, the submission of original manuscripts for publication. Writing a comprehensive thesis can take many months as a manuscript goes through a life cycle of reviews and edits by colleagues and supervisors. This allows graduate students to develop refined scientific writing skills in order to become proficient at translating research findings into comprehensive and clearly written concepts.

These skills can all be easily transferred to medical school, as many medical students will attempt to publish a research study or participate in medical writing and editing for a student publication. Medical students may submit original manuscripts to student-run medical journals and magazines. For example, the *University of Toronto Medical Journal* (UTMJ)[13], the Harvard Medical Student Review (HMSR)[14] and the Stanford Medicine Magazine[15] accept original and review pieces from medical students across Canada and the US. Medical student-produced textbooks such as *Toronto Notes*[16] have also garnered tremendous success over the past few years and offer an opportunity for involvement.

Lastly, medical students' opinions on educational and medico-social issues are highly valued by the medical education community. Medical students increasingly use opinion pieces, commentaries, and position papers as a method of communication with the public and medical professionals on current issues related to medical education and practice. Articulating arguments with clear supporting evidence will allow medical student writers to engage readers in critical thinking and dialogue for reform.

The section above highlights only a few of the many benefits that graduate degrees hold for aspiring medical students. Whatever your path to medical school may be, an advanced degree in the sciences will nearly always prove itself an asset throughout your professional journey in medicine.

---

[13] University of Toronto Medical Journal.
[14] Harvard Medical Students Review.
[15] Stanford Medicine Magazine.
[16] Toronto Notes, a study resource for Canadian Medical Licensing Exam.

6.3 Pharmacy

By Kevin Ren, HBSc, MD (Class of 2013)

Kevin obtained his HBSc in Physiology at the University of Toronto in 2008. He then completed a year of pharmacy at the University of Toronto before pursuing his MD at Queen's University (Class of 2013). Kevin is currently an Anatomical Pathology resident at Queen's (Class of 2018). Here he shares the reasons behind choosing each step of his academic career.

During undergraduate studies, I was one of those students who entered university with an open mind, but did not specifically know what to pursue as a career. After exploring different areas including the life sciences, physics, and art history, I developed an interest in the biological sciences. I chose to specialize in physiology because the physiology program offered a variety of laboratory oriented courses and provided a lot of hands-on experience. The University of Toronto also had excellent research opportunities, and I was able to enroll in the Research Opportunity Program (ROP) to spend a year learning experimental skills in neurophysiology. During these research experiences, I became quite fascinated with the ability of pharmaceutical agents to change animal and human physiology.

I had always wanted to apply the knowledge that I learned in labs and lecture halls to real life situations. Specifically, with a physiology background, I was interested in understanding how medications affect people. Pharmacy training offered exactly that and provided many other business and research opportunities. All of these compelling reasons made me pursue training in pharmacy.

After submitting my application to pharmacy, I took a very popular anatomy and histology course at the University of Toronto taught by an exceptional professor, who also ran the anatomy and histology curriculum for Toronto medical students. It still ranks as one of the best courses that I have ever taken. What fascinated me was how my professor was able to connect the dots between structure (anatomy and histology) and function (physiology) and ultimately branch that to clinical medicine. It became apparent to me that a career in medicine offered the complete and integrated training I desired. It involved assessing patients, interpreting test results, making diagnoses, and selecting treatments. Physicians are also trained as leaders in our health care system to make important decisions at critical moments. The profession demands a tremendous amount of responsibility and is showered with great respect in return.

Chapter 7: International students

7.1 Studying medicine in North America as an international student

By Sameer Masood, HBSc, MD

Sameer completed his undergraduate studies at the University of Toronto as an international student. He subsequently went on to graduate from the MD program at the University of Toronto as an international student and matched to the highly competitive Emergency Medicine residency program at the same institution. To further develop his international education experience, he will be pursuing a Masters of Public Health at Harvard University (Class of 2017). Here, he explains the reasons for coming to Canada for post-secondary education and discusses the challenges he had to overcome as an international student studying medicine in North America.

I arrived in Canada from Saudi Arabia for post-secondary education because of Canada's excellent academic reputation internationally. Canada has three of the top 30 medical schools globally[17] and studying at top schools in Canada is more affordable than similar schools in the US or the UK. I understood that to obtain a medical degree in Canada, it would be critical to complete an undergraduate degree in North America. Canada also encourages its students to consider settling down in the country by giving immigration preferences to those with Canadian educational backgrounds.

---

[17]QS Top Universities.

I am often asked what the biggest challenge was during this whole process. As an international student, you are often competing with domestic students for the same academic and non-academic goals. However, you are at a significant disadvantage due to cultural, financial, social, or at times immigration-related barriers. For example, there were instances where I was not eligible for a scholarship or opportunity due to my status as an international student, despite being one of the most qualified candidates.

My advice for international students is to find mentors (preferably with an international background) early in their journey that can guide and help them through barriers that only international students may face and understand. It is already a tremendous investment in time and money to study abroad, so you want to make this process as smooth as possible. It is vital to be able to find an international student who has already accomplished what you are embarking upon. Furthermore, I cannot over-emphasize the importance of doing your research before deciding which school to attend for undergraduate studies. In fact, I would even suggest that it is essential to incorporate potential barriers to entering medical school while planning your post-secondary education, as your path to medical school will certainly be influenced by your decision to attend a certain school for undergraduate studies. Lastly, it is important to remember that while you do face additional challenges as an international student, you also bring unique skills and experiences that are unparalleled, and it is up to you to turn these experiences into strengths. I had to create my own path to get to where I am and certainly had my fair share of challenges in doing so.

7.2 Obtaining a study visa

By Vincent Wong, BComm, JD

Vincent obtained his Bachelor of Commerce and Juris Doctor Degrees from the University of Toronto in 2010 and 2013 respectively. He currently works as a lawyer at the Metro Toronto Legal Clinic, which offers legal aid to newcomers to Canada, who may otherwise experience difficulty navigating through the legal system due to cultural and language barriers. He is also the owner of VW Law, a small firm that specializes in visa and immigration services.

To study in a foreign country, one would need to obtain a study visa. Although the application details may vary depending on the country of interest, the general application requirements remain much the same. For example, to study in Canada as an international student, you will need to obtain a study visa from Citizenship and Immigration Canada (CIC). After you finish your program of study, you may be interested in staying in Canada to work or to immigrate permanently and become a Canadian permanent resident. Immigration and visa issues are often complicated, and applicants should be extremely careful about following immigration rules and regulations.

Before you can apply for a study visa, you must have been accepted at a designated learning institution (DLI) in Canada. You may use the DLI link[18] to browse potential learning institutions or decide if a particular learning institution is duly designated before applying for enrollment. Each DLI has a

---

[18] Citizenship and Immigration of Canada. Designated Study Institution list.

unique DLI number that should be indicated on the study visa application. In addition, you need the following documents to apply for a study visa:

1. Proof of acceptance

If you plan to attend any school (primary or secondary), college, university, or other educational institution in Canada, the school must complete and send you a letter of acceptance. You must include the original letter with your study permit application.

2. Proof of identity

You must provide a valid passport or travel document for you and each accompanying family member. The passport or travel document must allow you to return to the country that issued it. Citizens of the United States do not need a passport, but rather a documentation to prove citizenship or permanent residence.

3. Proof of financial support

You must prove that you can support yourself and the family members who accompany you while you are in Canada. This may be provided in a variety of ways, such as proof of a Canadian bank account in your name, if money has been transferred to Canada.

4. Letter of explanation

In some cases, you may wish to apply for a study permit even if you do not need one right away. There are benefits to having a study permit, even if you do not require one. For example, if you decide to continue studying in Canada later on, you can apply to renew your study permit from within Canada. This may involve a letter of explanation describing your intent to continue studying. Otherwise, if you wish to continue studying in the country but your study permit has expired, you must apply through a Canadian visa office outside Canada.

Chapter 8: Interviews

8.1 Medical school interviews

By Rosa Lee, HBSc, MD Candidate (Class of 2018)

Rosa obtained her HBSc from McMaster University. She is a medical student at Queen's University in Kingston (Class of 2018). She has had extensive experiences with mentoring pre-medical students, which includes teaching the MCAT, founding and chairing numerous non-for-profit health organizations in Canada, and speaking at various career mentorship events. In this section, she discusses interview formats and tips for success.

Getting an interview is itself is an accomplishment. Now that you have gotten to this final and the *most important*, stage, how can you seize the opportunity and reach closer to becoming a doctor?

Twin traps of under and over-preparation

When I was asking around for tips and advice to prepare for my medical school interviews a few years ago, there was one response I always got: *be yourself.* This can be frustrating advice to an interviewee who wonders: "Be myself, but how?" "What if being myself is not good enough?" and "What does *being myself* even mean?" As candidates, we tend to long for specific strategies to maximize chances, not leaving it to good faith.

At the time, I too did not understand what "being myself" meant, but having been on the other side as an interviewer, it is much clearer. I now realize that it is indeed important to "be yourself."

Here are some ways you can "be yourself:"

- Understand that there are no "*right* responses," only "*your* response."
  - Caveat: there are *wrong* answers, however. This is true particularly for questions/ stations testing ethics. Wrong answers are those that raise red flags. You must develop a mindset with lots of practice and answer ethical questions such that these red flags would not be a concern in the first place.

- Since there is no "right answer," there is no point memorizing or reciting responses. Interviewers want to know you, not your ability to recite others' responses.

- Those who give interviewers what they believe are the "correct or ideal response" will come across as robotic. In contrast, those who give answers that reveal their unique character will come across as human.

- Make it conversational.
  - Maintain professionalism, but at the same time, understand that your interviewers have seen many applicants. Be interesting, be engaging, and be conversational.

- Be honest. Interviewers can tell!

Other general tips

- Make yourself marketable: What is your selling point? What makes you unique?

- Show that you are well-rounded and that you can handle the rigors of medical training (e.g. How have you demonstrated resiliency in the past?)

- Build an "example bank" of experiences that have shown you have demonstrated certain qualities of a physician. Interviews questions tend to include a significant number of behavioral questions that are based on the premise that past performance predicts future performance.

- Being able to understand various perspectives on an issue (e.g. given a medical scenario, you should be able to think from the perspectives of a patient, the patient's family, the physician, hospital, and the healthcare system).

- Know why you want to be a doctor.
    - Have you considered other careers?
    - Do you know what being a doctor consists of and have you done observerships with physicians?
    - Why you would like to be a doctor and not another related profession)?

Specific tips for the Multiple Mini Interview (MMI)[19]

- Become comfortable with the MMI setting.
    - Although over-preparing could be fatal when it comes to memorizing content, I would suggest practicing MMI stations just to get familiar with and confident in the MMI setting.
- Get diverse opinions.
    - Pre-medical students are a unique subgroup of people, and getting opinions only from other candidates may bias your view. Get opinions from medical students, physicians and other health professionals if possible. Get opinions from those who have no relationship to healthcare whatsoever.

Specific tips for traditional interviews

- Know yourself.
    - This is where your holistic self, your personal stories, and your brand will shine. Reflect on your experiences and think about the image that you want to portray to your interviewers.
- Make sure you know your application and have a few experiences to highlight.
    - Activity lists, supplementary essays, research projects, etc.
- Research the school and the program.

---

[19]McMaster Medical School: Admissions manual for interviewers.

- You should already know why the program should want you, but why do *you* want them? What aspect of the program appeals to you?

Topics to explore

Below are some topics worth exploring. There is no point in memorizing names and dates, but being capable of discussing the following subjects may come in handy:

- The healthcare system and different models in other parts of the world

- Ethical principles guiding medical practice

    - Know ethics! If you never took a medical ethics course, consider reading *Doing Right* by Philip C. Hebert.[20] It is important to understand and recognize the main ethical principles guiding medicine and to apply them during your MMI as necessary.

    - Review the Hippocratic Oath[21] – the modern version is still very much relevant.

- Top global health issues and role of the World Health Organization (WHO)

- Currently relevant controversial issues in medicine

- Basic law governing medical practice

- Different specialties in medicine

---

[20] Philip C. Herbert (2014). Doing Right: A Practical Guide to Ethics for Medical Trainees and Physicians. Third Edition. Oxford University Press.
[21] Johns Hopkin's University.

Know the medical curriculum and physician competencies.

Medical schools orient their curricula based on standards that national medical colleges set for their doctors. For the Canadian system, this standard is the "CanMEDS" model.[22] In other words, schools *want* candidates with demonstrated potential in each of the CanMEDS competencies. Review them and think about how you can show your potential in each (Hint: how have your experiences prepared you for those roles? What leadership roles have you taken? How have you enhanced your ability to communicate effectively? Do you have research skills, academic scholarships, or other experiences that pushed you as a scholar?)

In 2015, the role "manager" has changed to "leader". This shows the increasing demand for leadership skills amongst Canadian physicians.

---

[22] Royal College of Physicians and Surgeons of Canada. CanMEDS Framework.

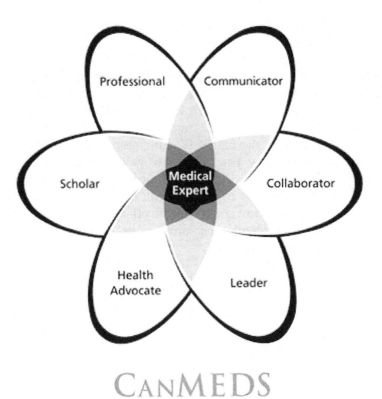

Chapter 9: Medical school and beyond

9.1 The medical school curriculum and residency match

By Jiayi Hu, HBSc, MD

Most medical schools in North America have four-year programs. McMaster University and the University of Calgary in Canada are two notable exceptions, both with a three-year accelerated program with limited summer breaks. In Canada, regardless of your school, the training process is well standardized. In the US, however, there are over 100 schools and the quality of education may be quite variable. You would have to complete the same set of national board exams to be eligible for independent practice in either Canada or the US.

Typically, the first half of the medical school curriculum involves mostly didactic lectures with relatively limited patient exposure. This time block is usually called "pre-clerkship" and it has the goal of building a strong knowledge foundation in the mechanisms, manifestations, and management of various diseases. Other topics that are commonly covered include anatomy, histology, and embryology.

The second half of medical school is termed "clerkship," during which all students complete clinical rotations and participate in patient care for integrated clinical learning. The core rotations include internal medicine, surgery, family and community medicine, obstetrics and gynaecology, paediatrics, and psychiatry. Other core rotations may include anaesthesia, emergency medicine, ophthalmology, or otolaryngology, depending on the school.

Other than core rotations, students also have elective rotations during which they have the opportunity to complete rotations in any specialty. This is either for career exploration or to prepare one for residency applications in their specialty of interest. It is usually a three-month period with rotation every two weeks (individual schools may vary).

During the last year of medical school, students apply for residency positions, which determine their future specialty of practice. In Canada, there are usually over 2,000 domestic applicants per year for roughly the same number of residency spots[23]. At the same time, there is also a similar volume of international applicants (those who trained abroad and are Canadian permanent residents or citizens) for only one tenth of the available spots. Different specialties also have varying levels of competitiveness. Generally speaking, over 90% of domestic applicants match to a spot, and over 70% can obtain their first choice specialty, but not necessarily at their first choice school[21]. Should a medical student not be successful in the matching process, one can still participate in the second and final round of applications (the second match), or wait until the next application cycle. Most career counselors advise students to apply broadly in the first round to avoid disappointment, as the second match round is significantly more competitive.

---

[23] Canadian Resident Matching Services.

9.2 Matching to Canada for residency as a US medical student

By Yale Wang, HBSc, MD (Class of 2015)

Yale obtained his HBSc and MSc in Laboratory Medicine and Pathobiology at the University of Toronto. He then completed this MD from St. Louis University in the United States. Yale achieved a score of 260 on the USMLE (United States Medical Licensing Exam) Step 1, which placed him in the top 3rd percentile of participants. He is currently a Family Medicine resident in Toronto (Class of 2017).

A popular question I am often asked is: "Were you considered a Canadian Medical Graduate (CMG) when matching to Canada?" I am glad to tell you yes! If you are Canadian (citizen or permanent resident) and attended an LCME accredited medical school in the USA (i.e. the vast majority of schools in the continental USA)[24], then you are considered a CMG because the LCME also accredits Canadian medical schools. It means you take the same exam as Canadian medical graduates to qualify for practice licensure. If you strongly wish to match back to Canada for residency, I would suggest you that apply to all programs that you are willing to pursue.

Another question I am asked is: "Does your USMLE score matter for residency matching?" I would say the answer is both "no" and "yes." "No" because you are not evaluated by your USMLE score. In fact, you do not even need to report it as part of your application. Nobody would notice that you neglected to

---

[24] Liaison Committee On Medical Education (LCME) Medical School Directory.

put something there, and nobody would care even if you have an amazing score. However, the answer would be "yes" in that you want to leave yourself with a backup plan in case you do not match in Canada, especially if you are applying to a competitive specialty. I have seen very competitive candidates fail to match to Family Medicine, which has the greatest number of spots in Canada. Having a strong USMLE score would significantly strengthen your residency application in the US.

One challenge of pursuing medical education in the US is that it can be very expensive (usually at least twice as expensive as Canada). To finance the high tuition fees, you can turn to government assistance, private lending, and banking institutions, for a total of usually of up to $250,000 in financial support. Not all the money is available immediately, however, and some schools may require full tuition to be paid up front.

I think my US medical education prepared me somewhat well to adapt to Canadian residency training. It has given me a stronger knowledge base in the basic sciences and in disease pathophysiology, which is heavily examined on the USMLE. As a result, I was well prepared for electives in Emergency Medicine and non-patient care specialties such as pathology, where the demands for knowledge are high. However, having trained in a different system, I find that Canadian students usually possess stronger hands-on skills and case presentation skills. I was not prepared to write daily orders, arrange admissions, and dictate consult notes when I first came back to Canada for elective rotations. Perhaps, it takes time to adjust to a new system and environment. Nonetheless, the Canadian training programs and licensure exams ensure that all candidates reach a required level of competency at the end of their training.

9.3 Residency and fellowship

By Jiayi Hu, Sameer Masood, and Manveen Puri

The duration of residency training may vary depending on the specific medical system in which one trains. In Canada, residency can last from two to six years or longer if one wishes to pursue a post-graduate degree at the same time. In addition, fellowship opportunities are available after residency for further clinical or career development. Here, we will discuss three residency streams as examples to highlight differences in program design and career prospectus.

1. Plastic Surgery

Plastic surgery residency, like most surgery programs, is a five-year program through the Royal College of Physicians of Canada. The first two years involve rotations in other specialties, such as general surgery and orthopedic surgery, to attain a fundamental level of clinical competency before progressing to senior level training that is focused on plastic surgery.

The day usually begins at 7 am or earlier with rounding on patients, followed by daily clinical activities at 8 am such as operations, minor procedures, or clinics. The day concludes at 5-6 pm after all patient and emergency issues have been addressed. Typically, there is an on-call resident every day to manage any patient issues that arise overnight. There is also usually dedicated formal teaching days every week, as well as informal teaching sessions during clinical encounters.

At the end of residency, one may choose to work in the following settings: academic, community, and private practice. Many residents choose to take on fellowship training to further develop and refine their skills, as well as to strengthen their job prospects. For plastic surgery, fellowship options may include subspecialties in hand surgery, craniofacial surgery, and paediatrics.

2. Emergency Medicine

Specialist training in Emergency Medicine is a five-year program in Canada through the Royal College of Physicians of Canada and four years in the US. There is also an option to pursue emergency medicine training through family medicine. Since emergency medicine is a broad field that encompasses aspects of virtually all the areas of medicine, the practice involves a significant amount of non-emergency medicine training i.e. surgical rotations, paediatrics, psychiatry, gynecology, etc. Like most training programs, there is graduated learning and responsibility, and the training focuses on emergency medicine solely in the senior years.

Most programs offer an option to pursue additional training in the 4th year of the program. A variety of opportunities exist and residents may choose to pursue additional clinical training in the form of a fellowship (critical care, ultrasound, toxicology, etc.), additional post-graduate education such as a Master's degree in education, research, etc., or a research fellowship amongst other options.

Clinical work is predominantly shift based (usually 8-10 hour shifts) and can be at an academic or a community hospital. The scope of practice is extremely broad and includes acutely ill patients requiring resuscitation, such as trauma patients or patients with life-threatening organ failures, paediatric patients, psychiatric patients, and patients with a variety of common minor problems. Hence, as an ER physician, one must be able to have excellent decision-making skills and great problem-solving abilities.

Beyond clinical work, there is a variety of options available such as clinical teaching, simulation training, quality improvement, and other administrative positions.

3. Family Medicine

Since the early 1990s, Family Medicine in Canada has been a specialty with its' unique two-year residency program. Prior to this, all medical school graduates completed a "rotating internship" year and were qualified as "General Practitioners (GPs)," a model that continues to exist in many parts of the world. The creation of a separate residency program was born out of the increasingly complex skills required to practice Family Medicine successfully.

Family Medicine in Canada is also unique because of the vast disparity in health human resources between rural and urban areas. The lack of traditional "specialists" in many rural communities results in vastly different scopes of practice. Outside the family medicine clinic, family physicians in Canada may find themselves providing care in many other settings including emergency medicine, obstetrics, hospitalist medicine (care of inpatients), palliative care, anaesthesia, and surgical assists. Also, many family physicians practice in an area of special focus because of personal interest or the needs of a given community. Examples of focused practices include travel medicine, pain medicine, sports medicine, cosmetic medicine, and hospice care. The list is as long as the variety of patients that family physicians encounter. Underlying this diversity is the principle that family physicians are specialists in general practice, that is, the care of the undifferentiated patient.

Given this flexibility, the two-year residency program has become increasingly competitive in recent years. Programs vary in design across institutions, but have family medicine as their base plus a broad range of core rotations in areas such as pediatrics, psychiatry, obstetrics, internal medicine, and emergency medicine. There is also elective time to explore practicing in a particular setting or area of focus. Residents who are interested in receiving additional training in an area of interest also may apply to various programs such as emergency medicine, hospitalist medicine, and sports medicine for a fellowship or "plus one" year.

9.4 Working as a Medical Officer in the military

By Manveen Puri, HBSc, MD, CCFP, MPA Candidate (Class of 2018)

Manveen is a Medical Officer with the Canadian Armed Forces. He enrolled in the Medical Officer Training Program (MOTP) during his third year of medical school and is currently posted to 2 Field Ambulance in Petawawa, Canada. He is also pursuing a part-time Master of Public Administration degree at the Royal Military College of Canada in Kingston.

Since antiquity, militaries have required the expertise of physicians and healers to help take care of the wounded. The Medical Officer role exists in most modern militaries in some form, but can vary substantiality from nation to nation. My experience is with the Canadian Armed Forces, which represents a unique environment in which you can practice medicine. As a Medical Officer, you provide medical care for military members at a base in Canada or abroad during war time or on peacekeeping and humanitarian missions.

Military medicine is quite different from regular family practice. There is a large emphasis on preventative health, occupational medicine, sports medicine, and psychiatry. Depending on operational requirements, many Medical Officers also undergo extra training in Flight and/or Dive medicine. In addition, many military physicians also "moonlight" in the civilian healthcare system, and work at their local Emergency Department. This opportunity to work in the Canadian Forces' federal system as well as your local provincial system gives you a unique vantage point into many of the challenges facing each system, as well as where opportunities for innovation lie.

As a Canadian pre-medical student interested in this path, you must first secure admission to a Canadian medical school. You must then apply to the Canadian Forces under the Medical Officer Training Program (MOTP). If you are already in the military, you must apply through the Military Medical Training Plan (MMTP). Once accepted, the military will pay for medical school as well as pay you a salary. In return, you incur a 3-5 year return of service obligation. Both entry plans currently require you to complete a residency in Family Medicine. There are minimal military commitments during medical school and residency. Once you are fully trained, you start working full-time with the military. You will be posted to a Canadian Forces base in Canada, which will be your home unit for the next few years. Much of your first year will be spent doing military courses where you will become acquainted with the role of an Officer in general, and then more specifically with the role of a Medical Officer. In other words, you will be a "dual professional." This is a commitment that cannot be taken lightly, and it is important to determine whether the military as an organization fits your values, beliefs, and lifestyle choices. It is also important to realize that the military is a large organization and that physicians are a small part of a much larger family. Succeeding as a military physician will require you to accept your role with humility and understand that it is not about you. Rather, your role is to support the troops and assist military commanders in executing their operational missions.

In return for this heavy responsibility, military physicians are presented with many unique opportunities to participate in deployments and take part in exercises with Canada's allies throughout the world. The military also places immense importance on leadership development and invests lots of time and money in its personnel to develop and nurture leadership skills. After 3-5 years of service, you may also have the opportunity to apply for further post-graduate training in select residences such as general surgery, orthopedic surgery, internal medicine, radiology, and psychiatry. In all, a career in the military can be extremely rewarding for the right individual. Like any career, succeeding is part hard work and part luck i.e. "being at the right place at the time."

9.5 Physician turned entrepreneur

By Joshua Liu, BSc, MD

Joshua received his BSc in Biology from York University in 2009 and his MD from the University of Toronto in 2013. He is currently the CEO of Seamless Mobile Health and has been the recipient of multiple prestigious awards, including the Canadian Top 20 under 20 and Forbes Top 30 under 30 in Healthcare. He will be discussing his career transition from physician to entrepreneur.

During my medical training, I became very interested in broader health system problems, and the way emerging technologies (e.g. mobile technology) could be used to better engage and monitor patients outside the hospital setting. I saw firsthand the barriers faced by healthcare organizations in trying to build and scale technology across the health system. I wanted to make as big an impact as possible, and I believed a start-up company would be the best vehicle to deliver healthcare innovation that could scale.

I would say the most important skill by far is focus. Focus on fewer priorities. Focus on optimizing fewer metrics. Focus on the few important tasks that create the most value. Say "No" to everything else that detracts you and your team from the core focus. It is already hard enough to do one thing well. The second requirement is simply an extremely high work ethic. Intelligence, talent, and skill are essential ingredients, but nothing will help you move as quickly as just working harder than everyone else works.

One thing I want to share with undergraduate students is that predicting the future is hard. Your career change can be dynamic, and you should have the ability to adapt to new paths and environments. I would not have expected to be working in a tech company full-time this soon. If I did, I would have spent more time learning to program and understand the tech industry. In my opinion, if we are talking purely about job prospects, an undergrad degree in computer science/engineering will continue to provide the best possible opportunities in every industry over the next 10-20 years.

That said, I also think we will see a dramatic shift in the utility of traditional education in the workforce. What is increasingly important is not going to be what you did your degree in (or if you did one at all), but what proven knowledge and/or skills you have, whether you learned that in school or on your own. One can pursue multiple career paths after medical education. For me, entrepreneurship was my passion and, therefore, a foundation in software, engineering, and design would make me highly valuable in one of the fastest growing industries today. You should reflect on what unique experiences would help you to better develop your career.

Chapter 10: Building your soft skills

By Aly Madhavji, CPA, CA, CMA, CIM

Aly received his BComm with Distinction from the University of Toronto in 2012 and he is currently pursuing his Masters of Business Administration (MBA) from INSEAD. He is an international award-winning author, motivational speaker, and community builder. He will be discussing how to build your soft skills.

10.1 Personal branding

Your personal brand is the image you portray externally, which gives others insight into your reputation, experience, and identity. It is formed based on a combination of social media, personal interactions, pieces of work, and word-of-mouth. Your personal brand is crucially important leading up to and following medical school because it is used to conceive notions about you. Since personal branding on social media is more controllable, it is wise to develop your personal brand consciously through Facebook, blogs, Twitter, LinkedIn, and other social media outlets. For example, using Facebook, make sure there's nothing you would not want an individual or a member of the admissions team to see. On blogs and Twitter, you can share your viewpoints with the world, but ensure that you are not violating the points of view of others. Using LinkedIn, you can share your work and volunteer experience, passionate causes, skills, and even obtain recommendations and endorsements to provide a more holistic external image. You can share your interests and passion through all of these tools, and it will help with developing connections, seeking mentors, experiential opportunities, and your medical school admissions.

Developing your personal brand is a work in progress. A good starting point is to spend some time searching through your social media connections and network for role-model profiles and brands that you believe are good examples. It will help you to envision some of the short to medium term possibilities for each social media platform. Personal branding is an area that you can focus on developing during your undergraduate studies and before medical school, but do not forget that it is a continuous work in progress over the entire span of your career!

For more advanced users, you can start a personal website, which could include a blog, photos, videos, and other interesting things to share. This is optional since you can have a similar impact on existing social media platforms.

10.2 How to network

Learning how to network effectively is one of the most important skills you can build during and following your undergraduate studies to prepare you for a successful career. Networking can help you gather insight into medical school admissions, life during medical school, specializations, residency, the profession, the lifestyle, and many other important matters. Having a flexible and thoughtful approach to networking can help you maximize your results.

Here's **Aly's 5-Step Networking Formula**, which is adapted and enhanced from the Networking section of his international award-winning book 'Your Guide to Succeed in University':

1) Network up & down

It's all about creating strong connections and relationships with individuals at all levels and stages of their career. Many people try to target experienced doctors, but it is wise to meet experienced professionals as well as individuals at a similar progress level or even less experienced than you. The reason for this is because any one of your connections could help you form new relationships, find a strategic mentor, or with advice related to medical school or beyond.

2) Help others including your "competition"

This likely seems counterintuitive to help people you perceive as your competition, which may be fellow undergraduate classmates or other medical school applicants. However, this separates you from everyone else. For example, if you help to introduce connections, build relationships, and have good intentions you will stand out from the crowd, and whether that's to an individual, a doctor, a potential mentor, or a member of an admissions team, there will be a lasting positive impression.

3) Make friends not "networks"

It is quite common that individuals use networking as an avenue to take rather than to build a smooth two-way relationship. However, if you begin with the intent of building a friendship, the relationship will naturally be a bilateral relationship, a give and take, which will result in more opportunities down the road and better prospects for your medical school admission.

4) Be yourself but don't be nervous

Some prospective medical school students are nervous while talking to current medical school students, members of the faculty or admissions teams, medical doctors, or other highly accomplished individuals. However, it's important to be yourself, find common topics of interest and to consider every moment as a learning opportunity. It is a continuous development process, so make sure you reflect at the end of each day on how you will improve the next day.

5) Solidify the connection

It is always important to ask for a business card and to connect with your new contacts via LinkedIn, even follow them via Twitter. If it is a more formal connection, you can send them an email and connect via LinkedIn. If it's less formal, you can add them with a short LinkedIn message or even follow and tweet at them! It's critical to solidify your new relationship by mentioning a couple of details discussed during your conversation. You can also suggest scheduling a time to meet, perhaps over a coffee, to continue developing your newly formed connection. Remember that sending a Facebook request may not be appropriate; depending on your conversation, you can be the judge!

For more advanced networkers, LinkedIn can be used to expand your network through effective targeting. For example, using targeted searches to identify admissions staff, students, and faculty members at particular institutions and then sending a personalized introductory message seeking guidance over a coffee or phone call is a worthwhile strategy. Do not expect a very high response rate, but the connections you do make can be very valuable. When utilizing this approach, try to develop a template for your targeted messages and then tailor it for each contact, this will significantly improve your efficiency and effectiveness.

10.3 Take a leap of faith & learn how to bounce back from failure

The medical school admissions process is complicated, and it goes beyond academics; it's about your entire portfolio of what you bring to the table. This will also include your work and volunteer experience, causes that you are passionate about and other selling points that are relevant to the medical school admissions committee. When you review your work and volunteer experience, think of the vision that you are trying to share with the review committee. Try to look objectively at your personal brand. What are some of your strengths? What are some of your weaknesses? Think about how you can enhance your strengths and overcome your weaknesses.

You will likely have to try new experiences and pursue opportunities you never thought you could do. This may be during or following your undergraduate studies. You can try leading a student group, organize a social-development related volunteer opportunity, or a large-scale fundraiser for a passionate cause even if you think you might fail. Failure is one of the most valuable lessons you can learn, including how to build resiliency from those failures and to bounce back stronger each time.

The opportunity to take risks and to pursue certain demanding but rewarding goals is best during your undergraduate studies, even though you may believe your time is quite limited. It is important to make this a balancing act of finding the time to invest in worthwhile initiatives. Set challenging goals for yourself, even if you are unsure on how you will accomplish them. It's a win-win for you. If you succeed, you will develop beyond expectations, build confidence, and realize that you have accomplished something great. If you fail, it's tough, but you will learn an incredible amount from your mistakes, and it will significantly help your personal development.

When I was in the midst of my undergraduate studies, I took on some significant volunteer opportunities amounting to over 40+ hours a week while taking a full course load. At times, I struggled with balancing my schedule and would miss my classes to attend meetings and run events that I was passionate about. I tried to justify this to myself but after a number of poor interim grades, I realized that I was letting myself down academically. I ended up dropping some of these courses and considered it a significant personal failure. This was incredibly tough for me to overcome because exceeding your personal and academic goals is a vital part of university. I felt like this failure was a major low point for me. After taking some time to re-calibrate I worked to plan my time better and developed personal goals to attend all of my classes. However, at the same time, I planned to continue with these volunteer roles that I was passionate about.

Looking back, the experience and opportunities I gained through overcoming this personal failure, along with these volunteer opportunities, have played an immense role in my personal development. Ensuring that you are taking on challenges and getting out of your comfort zone will help you write your story. These are the types of challenges, experiences, and resiliency that program admissions committees value, but most importantly, that you will benefit from after overcoming adversity.

Top 10 take home messages

1. Getting into medical school is a difficult journey. Find out in advance what you need to succeed and do not give up without a fight.

2. Your grades are one of the most important components of the medical school application. Talk to friends, senior students, and mentors to optimize your program and course selection for premedical studies.

3. Try to start meaningful volunteer activities early. They are beneficial to your community and are an excellent opportunity to experience altruism which will have a tremendous positive impact on your personal growth and character.

4. Research experience helps tremendously with the medical school application as well as the development of non-academic skills. Learn how to choose an ideal research team. Set realistic expectations but work at your highest capacity.

5. Most medical schools require completion of a standardized exam. Know the syllabus, practice exam questions, and stick to your study schedule.

6. Learn to manage time between academics and extracurricular activities. It will be an invaluable skill in your

future career as a physician and leader, and it takes a lifetime to master.

7. Not all physicians pursue a traditional background during their premedical studies. Whatever your academic background, always reflect on the skills and life experiences you have learned which will benefit your medical career.

8. Try to "be your-best-self" during the interviews. Practice can make it perfect because interviewing skills are very trainable.

9. Obtaining a medical education opens many doors for career opportunities other than treating patients. Your career changes can be dynamic and you must be ready to adapt to new paths and environments.

10. Learn how to network efficiently and collaboratively. This skill is crucial for your future medical career and beyond.

References

1. Ontario Universities' Application Centre (OUAC). http://www.ouac.on.ca/statistics/med_app_stats

2. Simmenroth-Nayda A., Gorlich, Y., Medical school admission test: advantages for students whose parents are medical doctors? MBC Medical Education. 15: 81. 2015.

3. Gillon R., Medical ethics: four principles and plus attention to scope. British Medical Journal. 1994. 309: 184.

4. Association of American Medical Colleges. MCAT Essentials. http://aamc-orange.global.ssl.fastly.net/production/media/filer_public/4d/ce/4dce76d7-2109-4897-97ee-678d3b94c228/essentials_2016_-_final_2016-03-24.pdf

5. Association of American Medical Colleges. MCAT Content. http://www.aamc.org/students/download/377882/data/mcat2015-content.pdf

6. Sample study schedule. www.Guidetomed.com/mcat-study-schedule

7. Royal College of Physicians and Surgeons of Canada. CanMEDS Framework. http://www.royalcollege.ca/portal/page/portal/rc/canmeds/framework

8. "Lessons Learned: Reflections of Canadian Physician Leaders" and "Leading from the front: experiences of Canadian physician leaders." With Free e-versions of both books available here: http://www.cma.ca/En/Pages/resources.aspx

9. American Association for Physician Leadership: http://www.physicianleaders.org

10. Canadian Medical Association Physician Leadership Institute: http://www.cma.ca/En/Pages/physician-leadership-institute.aspx

11. When clinicians lead: http://www.mckinsey.com/insights/health_systems_and_services/when_clinicians_lead

12. Coaching Physicians to Become leaders: http://hbr.org/2013/10/coaching-physicians-to-become-leaders

13. University of Toronto Medical Journal. http://utmj.org

14. Harvard Medical Students Review. http://www.hmsreview.org

15. Stanford Medicine Magazine. http://stanmed.stanford.edu

16. Toronto Notes. http://www.torontonotes.ca

17. QS Top Universities. http://www.topuniversities.com/university-rankings/university-subject-rankings/2016/medicine - sorting=rank+region=+country=+faculty=+stars=false+search =

18. Citizenship and Immigration of Canada. Designated Study Institution list. http://www.cic.gc.ca/english/study/study-institutions-list.asp

19. McMaster Medical School: Admissions manual for interviewers http://fhs.mcmaster.ca/mdprog/documents/InterviewerManualFull2012-13forWEBSITE.pdf

20. Philip C. Herbert (2014). Doing Right: A Practical Guide to Ethics for Medical Trainees and Physicians. Third Edition. Oxford University Press.

21. Johns Hopkins University. http://guides.library.jhu.edu/c.php?g=202502&p=1335759

22. Royal College of Physicians and Surgeons of Canada. CanMEDS Framework. http://www.royalcollege.ca/portal/page/portal/rc/canmeds/framework

23. Canadian Resident Matching Services, http://www.carms.ca/en/data-and-reports/r-1/reports-2015

24. Liaison Committee On Medical Education (LCME) Medical School Directory, http://www.lcme.org/directory

About the authors

Jiayi Hu

Jiayi received his HBSc with High Distinction in Biochemistry and Pharmacology (2009) from the University of Toronto. He then went on to complete his Doctor of Medicine (M.D.) at the same institution in 2013. He is currently a resident in Plastic and Reconstructive Surgery at McMaster University.

Since the early stages of his undergraduate studies, Jiayi has been very passionate about research in both the basic sciences and clinical medicine. He was involved in numerous projects at the University of Toronto resulting in two publications in cancer research journals of high impact. One of his projects, which focused on re-purposing existing non-oncological medications for the treatment of leukemia, led to a patent. He has also worked at McGill University and the University of Cambridge to expand his knowledge and skillset in basic science research.

Jiayi has a strong interest in career counseling, particularly aimed at undergraduate life science and medical students. During his undergraduate years, he co-founded Magna est Veritas, a pre-medical club with a 90% success rate in medical school admissions. He is frequently invited to speak at various career events at the University of Toronto's Career Centre. Jiayi is also a founding partner at MD Consultants (www.mdconsultants.ca), a Canadian educational consulting company focused on helping students pursue a career in healthcare and establish a professional collaborativenetwork.

Jiayi's current academic interests are focused on clinical research in the field of Plastic Surgery. Specifically, he is interested in understanding the psychological and economic forces that shape the decision-making process of both patients and physicians. Jiayi has presented his work at international conferences and published in several top tier journals.

Manveen Puri

Manveen received his HBSc with High Distinction (Human Biology, Anthropology) in 2009 and Doctor of Medicine (M.D.) in 2013 from the University of Toronto. He then went on to complete residency training in Family Medicine at the same institution (CCFP, 2015). He is now pursuing a Master of Public Administration degree at the Royal Military College of Canada.

Manveen currently serves as a Medical Officer (Captain) with the Canadian Armed Forces and is a practicing Family Physician. He is posted to 2 Field Ambulance in Petawawa. He is also an attending Emergency Physician at Pembroke Regional Hospital and Deep River & District Hospital. In addition, he maintains a practice in Addictions Medicine in the Greater Toronto Area.

Manveen has taken on various leadership roles over the years. He has served on the University of Toronto's Governing Council where he was a member of the Business Board and the Planning & Budget Committee. During residency, Manveen was Chief Resident (Family Medicine) at Credit Valley Hospital in Mississauga. He has received both the Gordon Cressy Award and the Arbor Award for his continued contribution to the University of Toronto community.

Mentorship has always been important to Manveen who has benefited from the generosity of his mentors. Since 2009, he has been an active mentor to pre-medical students at his alma mater New College. His mentees have gone on to attend prestigious medical schools from McGill to Stanford. Manveen speaks regularly about his experiences in medicine with high school and undergraduate audiences. In addition, Manveen is the co-founder of MD Consultants (www.mdconsultants.ca), a professional network of medical students, residents, and attending physicians who provide consultancy services in areas ranging from professional school admissions to second opinions.

Sameer Masood

Sameer received his HBSc with High Distinction in Human Biology in 2009 from the University of Toronto. He subsequently went on to complete his Doctor of Medicine (M.D.) in 2013 as the only international student in his class and one of the few in the history of the Faculty of Medicine. Sameer is currently a Royal College Emergency Medicine Resident Physician at the University of Toronto and is scheduled to complete his specialty training in 2018. He is currently a graduate student at Harvard University where he is pursuing a Master's in Public Health with an emphasis on Innovation and Quality Improvement. Given his dual clinical and academic roles, Sameer splits his time between Canada and the United States.

During his many years at the University of Toronto, Sameer has also been extensively involved in student mentorship and community building. Sameer spent three years as a residence student counselor at the university and has been a recipient of numerous awards including the Jon. S. Dellandrea award for academic excellence and the New College Centennial Award for student leadership.

As an Emergency Medicine resident physician at the University of Toronto, Sameer has been extensively involved in medical education and research. He has served multiple terms as an interviewer on both the Undergraduate Medical Admissions Committee and the post-graduate Emergency Medicine Residency Training Committee. Sameer is also a founding partner at MD Consultants (www.mdconsultants.ca), a Canadian consulting company geared towards helping high school and undergraduate students pursue a career in healthcare.

Sameer's current professional interests include clinical research within Emergency Medicine and using digital technology based innovation to solve the growing needs of the Canadian Healthcare System. He has won national research awards in Emergency Medicine and has published in several top-tier journals.

Aly Madhavji

Aly received his BComm with Distinction in 2012 from the University of Toronto. He is a December 2016 Masters in Business Administration (MBA) Candidate at INSEAD based in France and Singapore. As the author of the #1 College book on Amazon, Aly continues to energize and develop tens of thousands of current and aspiring University and College students through speaking engagements and mentorship. His internationally acclaimed book, "Your Guide to Succeed in University" (www.SucceedinUniversity.com), is an Award-Winner of the 2015 International Book Awards. He has worked with organizations and educational institutions across Canada and globally and makes his book fully accessible to students at no cost.

Aly served as a Governor of the University of Toronto where he was a member of the Executive Committee and Academic Board of the institution. He has been very active in community building, having served on numerous boards. He expanded the Books with Wings initiative for the University of Toronto International Health Program (UTIHP) raising an estimated $15,000 for students in need around the world.

Aly spent two and a half years in the Assurance practice for PwC in Toronto and New York, where he led audits of multinational Canadian and US clients. Aly then joined the Management Consulting practice with PwC as a Senior Consultant working in Canada, the United States, Brazil, and the Caribbean. He worked closely on the strategic investments of large private equity firms, the creations of centers of excellence, turnarounds of emerging market companies, and role re-engineering to create efficiencies.

He holds the Chartered Professional Accountant (CPA), Chartered Accountant (CA), Certified Management Accountant (CMA), and the Chartered Investment Manager (CIM) Designations. Aly has been featured in The Medium and The Varsity newspapers, the Ismaili Magazine, Mississauga Magazine, and University of Toronto Press.

Made in the USA
Monee, IL
12 February 2020